TAINTED COFFEE WITH 3 TEASPOONS OF SUGAR

(CURDLED MILK OR VENOMOUS CREAMER OPTIONAL)

BY

DARCEL RANAY GIBSON

To the victims of abuse.

Do not give up on your dreams; keep

believing, because when you have

faith, circumstances do change.

COPYRIGHT

DEDICATION

"February 21, 2001's Prayer" is dedicated to my daughter. "Whispering Willows" is dedicated to my stepfather and my mother.

My stepfather passed away on August 20, 1998, and my mother was dealing with losing a spouse, so I wrote the poem on November 10, 1998.

I thank God for my siblings; when I cried and was in distress, they hugged and made me laugh. I appreciated the kind words from my doctors and their staff.

The year 1998 was especially trying; my mother spent her days comforting my stepfather as he was dying, and my father was dealing with his own struggles.

ACKNOWLEDGMENT

I want to thank my Heavenly Father, who pulled me out of abusive situations and gave me love, peace, and joy.

I want to thank my daughter. Without her support, I would not have followed through with getting it published.

She is a college graduate, a fantastic mother of two children, and a dog.

I also thank my second-grade English teacher at Memorial Elementary School, who said that I had a gift.

AUTHORS' BIO

Darcel Ranay Gibson is the Law Librarian, an actor, and a photographer. She received an MBA in Global Management and a Master's Certificate in Human Resource Management from the University of Phoenix, a BS in Applied Psychology / Organizational Behavior from Albright College, and an AA in Liberal Arts from Northampton County Community College.

She found her love for writing poetry and short stories in her second-grade English Class at Memorial Elementary School in Washington, New Jersey, and she will continue to write for years to come.

She has had some of her poems published, has collaborated with other artists to write plays, and has been in a few plays as well as background acting for a few films.

She does photography in her spare time and has had her photos exhibited in art galleries, such as Andakulova Gallery, Thomson Gallery, Casa Del Arte, Nicoleta Gallery, and Cipriarte Venezia Gallery.

Darcel Ranay Gibson resides in Pennsylvania with family. Tainted Coffee With 3 Teaspoons Of Sugar, Curdled Milk or Venomous Creamer Optional is a collection of poems with short stories about her personal experiences.

TABLE OF CONTENTS

BRANDS OF SUGAR

MISSING YOU

Grief is sorrow, but it can be complicated because it deals with distinct types of losses and emotions. Someone may experience anger when dealing with grief, while someone else may cope destructively or cry daily.

Whatever effects grief may have on a person, no one can pinpoint how a person may act when managing such pain associated with grief. We can only hope to find a solution to dealing with loss.

When I broke up with a boyfriend, walked away from a disagreement with a friend or relative, or suffered a death, it was like I was mourning because that relationship was gone, and I had to pick up the pieces of my life.

Relationships come and go in life. On July 3, 2012, the hardest moment was hearing the news that my brother, Romero, had been murdered.

I felt an emptiness because I would never see him on this earth again. It felt like a bad dream, and I knew I would no longer have that person making me laugh or walking me to work or telling me that he loved me unconditionally.

I couldn't think straight. I cried on and off for days. It was not just my brother who was gone, but one of my best friends. I would no longer see his smile coming through my apartment door or see him joke with his siblings and our mother.

What I have are good memories of our childhood and adulthood, and the memory of his murder and the trial that my family had to endure.

I find myself remembering all those days that we spent together. As children, we had some good times growing up in the small town of Washington, New Jersey, with a large family. We had the chance to play and have fun. Romero may have had personal issues that he had to deal with in his life, but his siblings loved him.

He was the first person to talk to me about forgiving anyone who hurt me and to treat everyone with kindness. In addition, we talked about faith. It was great having those talks in the morning because they made me think and take the steps to be a better person. Romero had a kind soul.

I know having him in my life for almost 45 years was a good thing because I will always have those memories, whether they were good or bad, I will keep them in my heart. I realized that Romero had been struggling with his personal issues, but those personal issues do not change the unconditional love that I had for my brother.

CHEAP MASCARA

Being a grandmother of two human children and one dog, my day has some challenges.

The first one is to figure out what to wear to work. The second is doing my hair and makeup. The third challenge is getting up out of bed to complete the first two challenges, but nothing prepared me for the biggest challenge: cheap mascara.

Let me tell you about this story of how I was yawning at work and how I blinked. This was not just an ordinary blink. I blinked both eyes once, but my right eyelashes were stuck together because of the cheap mascara that I had put on that morning.

I was freaking out trying to pull my eye open without messing up my mascara. Unfortunately, the worst part was that I blinked my eyes a second time, and my right eyelashes were stuck together again.

Just imagine yourself prying open your dog's mouth because they tried to eat a napkin. Well, this was simpler than that, but it was a struggle, using two fingers on my right hand to hold my head up while using two fingers on my left hand to pry open my right eye, trying not to mess up my makeup and preventing my contact from popping out.

I was disgusted with myself, realizing I had tried to save a couple of dollars only to end up in this situation. I wondered whether it was worth it. The answer was no!

I was just so cheap because I wanted to save on gas and add a couple of extra dollars in my pocket.

My eyelashes looked a little clumpy, and they did not look natural. Now, I will just pay a little more, so I do not have to deal with any situations like this again.

SEEING FROM A VICTIM'S POINT OF VIEW

I had never thought that closeness would ever come into a family. I remember a time when I had seen the closeness as a small child, but as years passed, it was gone. Everyone was searching for the answers and looking for the clues, feeling empty within.

How can anyone understand what one goes through in life?

Was this a message that a person wants answered? Everyone may have forgotten his or her faith. There was no need for it at the time, but as the tragedies kept piling up in our lives like a pile of old, moldy newspapers collecting dust in the corner, we realized that we could not face this world alone.

In this world, a child needs love and understanding from their family. No hatred was necessary to mend a broken heart. Sure, there were tears and sadness.

No one can complain about the past, but we need to change what is now, or we will never change the future. The only crime that happens in a family is that no one talks when they are angry.

The reason is that they may not want to admit they are wrong, nor do they want to discuss what is bothering them; instead, they just stop speaking to one another and close themselves off from the rest of the world.

As years passed, they realized that they had made a mistake, and they did not know how to change those bitter feelings that they had picked up.

They may never forgive the abuser(s). After all, they destroyed a part of their family that was so dear to them, but I found that God does care about what is going on in our lives. His love can mend broken hearts and bring families back together again.

A person cannot hold onto baggage. Sometimes, people do, and they forget exactly when to let go of all the pain. I often wonder what they are going through.

Will they let the pain go? Will they allow that pain to strangle their souls? Or will they walk around like zombies, not knowing which way to turn?

If that individual wanted to, they could pick up those broken pieces, get help, and not waste time.

How long are they going to avoid the pain? They love, even when they do not love themselves. They may take advantage of everyone around them, like spoiled brats begging for everything in the candy store and throwing tantrums when they do not get their way.

They do not need to fight to justify being dead wrong about things, but they may realize that they need to have faith to survive in a cruel world that has gotten so dark and cold.

They may be unforgiving. They may have picked up unhealthy habits through the years, such as becoming dependent on drugs, drinking, and using people. They may not have the strength to move forward in their lives, and they forget who they truly are.

When was the last time you saw yourself in the mirror for who you truly are? Did you cry because you have lived a life of bitterness or selfishness, and that cannot seem to take off the coat you made that is spiritually killing your soul?

One may forget how to pray. I have learned over the years about having pain. It can strangle you from within, and therefore, it may show up on your face, and it could destroy your health. No one can imagine anyone living his or her life alone in one brief period.

I AM DONE

I woke up with concerns on my mind that upset my stomach and sent it on a rollercoaster ride. With tears in my eyes, I prayed for answers like any person would, while exploring the new world around me.

I had to voice those concerns because all my life, people were telling me how I felt, or what I thought, and what my dreams were for my life. There was never a compromise because my voice was lost somewhere in the mix.

One day, I woke up. I was standing alone, treated like a doormat piece of trash, as if I didn't belong in public. It seemed like I was a disease rather than a human being. "Please Abuse Her!" was a label put on my back.

No one was there. I was getting stares and poor treatment. What could top that? The negative words left by different abusers who had come and gone covered my mind, body, and soul like an old musty rag that I tried to shake off, but the stench filled the air and lingered.

No matter how hard I tried, I could not get these abusers to stop because I did not have the courage to stand up to any of them. I started to feel empty and began questioning everything around me because nothing made sense.

I wanted to make a friend who did not abuse me. I was not looking for a love connection, but I was looking for a friend that I could trust and who would not use me. It is hard sometimes. So many times, I kept things to myself. I found that hard to do because no one can be an island, nor can a person avoid human contact.

One day, I realized that God had a greater plan for my life, so I left with the clothes on my back and began to live.

BAD DREAM

I have looked beyond

The shadows that lurk in the darkness

Trying to hold me captive in that cold grave of my room

No windows to escape from

Got to have escape from within

No food

No drink

My mind is going insane from these hunger pains.

I scream,

However, no one is there?

Time ticks away at my soul

As I am getting old

This cannot be.

Why is this happening?

Snakes and worms are crawling all over me,

Until I cannot breathe.

My eyes awaken.

Oh my God!

It was a bad dream.

THE NEWS

Looking out the window

Seeing sickness and disease,

Hatred and pain,

No one helps a fellowman,

As time goes by,

It is getting worse.

Deceit is the biggest crime.

Each night as I pray,

I wish for a better day.

The future is not looking well.

Wars! Hate crimes!

They are alike.

What is the purpose of seeing people die?

Joy is lost along the way.

Do not cry.

This will end.

The dirt and grime are swept away.

Kindness and love bring a new day.

SNAPPING TURTLE'S CHEW TOY

I have learned that losses can range from minor to major. When I was around nine years old, my sister, Anika, my brother Romero, and I were playing with a snapping turtle that our brother Joel had found in the backyard of the apartment building where we lived.

Anika was around five years old, Romero was six, Joel was about eight, and Braxsen was around seven.

Anika pulled the snapping turtle's tail. Unfortunately, my left wrist was right in front of the snapping turtle's mouth, and it bit me there. I swung the snapping turtle around like a rag doll, and it seemed like its grip tightened.

I was crying and screaming at the top of my lungs while Anika and Romero were laughing so hard they were in tears. Blood ran down my arm, and I felt like I was going to faint from trying to pry the snapping turtle off my left wrist. Finally, Joel and Braxsen came out of our apartment to help.

Joel took a stick and prodded the snapping turtle's rear end, and it let go of my wrist. Then our mother cleaned my wound and wrapped my left wrist. I was traumatized by the terrible experience; it had nearly bitten a major artery.

With all the excitement that afternoon, we went inside the house and ate dinner. My left wrist hurt, and I had bruising around the bite mark.

I slept with my left wrist on a pillow each night, and I had to wait for a couple of weeks before I could go swimming, lift anything, or play. The snapping turtle escaped that night and was never seen again.

FEBRUARY 26, 2001'S PRAYER

Dear God,

I am kneeling here before you because I wanted to tell you, "Thank you" for being with me. You are the only one who understands my situation. People do not understand what it is like to be a single parent. I realize that it is all right because someone loves me enough to hold me every second of the day.

I know the pain would be too much to bear if I lived that old life again. Lord, I was falling apart, and you saved me from that abusive relationship. I sit and pray that my daughter will have a healthy relationship.

I know that you love us and that you have a purpose for our lives. People would rather see us fall. I am one person who would like to see her child share time with her father figure, go to the movies, and so forth. I have done the job of two parents, and I have not stopped.

You have given me strength and hope for my life; I would not be where I am if I did not have you holding me up. Love gets me going, and peace lets my heart know I am alright.

CURDLED MILK OR VENOMOUS CREAMER IS OPTIONAL

FIRST TIME I WITNESSED HURT & PAIN

When I was three years old, an older white girl was pushing an empty swing by the Easton Boys & Girls Club on a sticky, hot summer's day.

As I was walking past, heading to the monkey bars, the metal piece of the swing caught the corner of my left eye, and my whole body felt as if it was lifted into the air before being dragged forward.

As the swing dragged my body, I could feel my flesh tearing as the blood poured out of the left side of my face like candy bursting out of a piñata. My left eye was just dangling out of the socket.

I did not realize that I was lying in my own pool of blood. I could not get up because I felt lightheaded, and my body felt like a limp noodle lying still on a plate.

I was not sure whether I would see my mother or anyone else in my family again; I felt like my life was slowly ending, so I lay there saying a quick prayer.

My Uncle Ervin jumped over the fence, scooped me up, and carried me home. I could hear my mother crying and screaming at the top of her lungs, wondering if I was going to live or die. Someone called for an ambulance.

I passed out from blood loss and did not realize that we had gotten to Easton Hospital. I managed to wake up a bit and saw my mother talking to one doctor, who told her that they couldn't save my left eye, but a visiting doctor said he could save it.

Then I saw this man comforting my mother, and I was trying to reach out to touch my mother's hand, but this was impossible. As the orderly was wheeling me into the operating room for surgery, I passed out cold.

When I woke up, I could see my body on the operating table with the doctors and nurses hovering over me while they were trying to save my eye and my life as best they could.

I heard a voice and walked into another room that was all white, with people draped in white clothes talking to one another, and a man sitting in a chair. The man in the chair called my name and told me that I should not be there because it was not my time, and I had to go back to my body. My soul pushed back into my body.

At that moment, I got up off the operating table as the doctor was still working on the left side of my face. I told them that God had healed me, and I was leaving. The doctors and nurses had to hold me down while the anesthesiologist administered something to put me to sleep, so the doctor could finish stitching me up.

Once the surgery was over, I was taken to my hospital room for a couple of days. For the first time, I was alone and afraid that my mother was not there to keep the boogeyman away. I said my prayers of gratitude that night because I realized I could see out of my left eye and that I could see my family.

After the older girl hit me with the swing, I saw that everyone in the neighborhood was outraged because she had been pushing an empty swing that struck the left side of my face.

These people wanted answers, but there was no one to give. The girl and her family moved without a forwarding address. For so many years, I wanted to tell that girl that I forgave her, and I know that pushing that swing as I walked by was not her fault because she was playing with the swings, as all kids do.

One mistake happened, and someone got hurt, but it was a lesson she had to live with for quite a few years.

MEANING OF LOVE

Love is having someone who cares about you, no matter what you have done wrong in your life. No one can take that feeling away from you. You want that feeling to stay, to grow, and to comfort you each day. Finally, love is letting go of all the regret, pain, and disappointment because they are no longer in your zip code.

WAKE UP CALL

You can close your eyes,

And see what you

Want to see.

But one day,

You must

Open your eyes,

And face

Reality.

DEAR ROMERO

I am writing this letter to you to tell you about so many things. I know how you wanted everyone to start calling you "Romero" because you wanted to leave the nickname "Alfred" behind. I am writing this letter to address you by your birth name.

I remember the day that you told the family how you wanted to leave the name "Alfred" behind because you wanted to start anew and leave the past behind. I wish you had gotten the opportunity to start what you wished for, but that was not how we planned.

I remember the day that you left, and I want to tell you that I love you and will miss you. I should tell you that I have moved to the apartment across the parking lot.

It was a good thing because I did not always hear the noise or any issues outside. I was grateful to have that third-floor apartment. It felt like I had my own little island. My new apartment was quiet, so I did not have to worry about noise.

I got my driver's license with the help of a driving school and the encouragement of one of my grandchildren. I know that you would be proud of me for taking that big leap of faith because it changed my life.

I did not have to rely on everyone around me for rides or to get to different places. I got a chance to meet so many different people along the way.

Would you believe that I had gone on four mission trips? I amazed myself. I did not think that I could do it because I was so scared and my self-esteem was low, but with faith, I managed to do it.

I have seen beautiful places, eaten great food, and met great people. The fear and the low self-esteem are gone. I have changed so much, and my faith has gotten stronger.

Would you believe that I started acting a couple of years ago? It has been an amazing ride. I did not think that I would enjoy it, but it gave me another way to express myself. I am so grateful that I found my voice.

I know this letter is short, but I wanted to tell you that I did not forget you and that you are always on my heart. One day we will see each other again.

Love you, brother.

PASS ME THE FREEDOM

Do not take the joy that lies within

The thing I found.

When I gave up sin,

The carpets once filled with

Dirt and grime,

Condemning me for a crime,

The Son who called my name.

Now, I live past the lies

All the rumors just die,

Bearing no life, no thought, or

Consciousness within.

I will stand alone,

With no one to say,

"Why don't you just die so we don't have to see your face?"

I will lie in the open field with freedom.

Stamped on my lip

CURDLED MILK

Abuse strangles innocent souls,

Destroying all the joy,

Killing every second.

Hatred seen in every word.

Death.

Is at the curb,

Leaving scars on every limb

Of the family tree.

There is that noose.

Swinging in the wind.

TRUTH

Care for me,

A withered soul

Lying in the bitter cold.

Cannot look back.

The pain is overflowing,

And it tries to strangle

That last breath.

I looked for life,

Around the bend,

Knowing I cannot pretend.

COMPASSION

Falling into an empty space,

Hoping for that sweet embrace,

All was hope,

And all was joy,

Finding wisdom within the darkness

Of the room.

Would life come my way?

For another day,

Holding me in your arms

Like a baby,

I feel safe,

All because of your amazing Grace.

SEEKING DREAMS

Some people have dreams,

That last a lifetime;

Those dreams fill their lives,

A destiny of fulfillment.

When not accomplishing them,

Some are left hurting and suffering,

While others at least try.

IMAGES

Poetry brings

A new experience

To our lives.

A BLANKET OF NEGATIVITY

I woke up terrified.

Of what is waiting for me?

At sunrise

Verbal abuse knocking on the door to let them in,

Physical abuse whispers sweet nothing in my ear.

As the milk curdles on the kitchen table

I am hiding in the bedroom closet.

Praying

Hoping

When will I be free of the torment from this man?

He claims that he loves me,

Choking me with each word,

Hitting me until I cannot see

The curdled milk that covers me like a blanket of negativity.

DYSFUNCTIONAL BEHAVIOR

The sun shines over the east side

Wondering what it must look like at sunrise.

Thinking of past hurts and comparing them to my current situation

Climbing out of that prison

Made of dysfunctional behavior from the mind of a psychopath.

MONSTER

A soul broken.

Nowhere to turn

Each fist hitting me in submission.

As I scream.

I lose consciousness.

Why? Why?

Caught up in this dysfunctional love.

Paying the price,

Each choke hold that I endure.

Each punch.

Each kick.

The nightmares that I envision each night.

Afraid to move a muscle.

As the tainted coffee flows through my veins,

The darkness creeps in,

Poisoning my mind until I'm blinded by his charm.

Unable to see.

What this monster has done to me!

FLAVORS OF COFFEE

ABUSE

Abuse is like feeding someone a spoonful of arsenic every day; each does flows through a person's veins, slowly killing the soul. Over time, that person becomes an empty shell. Once an empty shell, the person loses all hope, trust, faith, and the belief that love can exist in their life.

They will always keep their guard up because of trust issues. The person keeps special moments to themselves because sharing them becomes a torturous interrogation, why anyone would have you at any function.

The person cannot always tell those dark secrets because doing so rehashes the pain that the pain of mental, physical, and emotional abuse they try so desperately to hide.

Abusers assume they know their victims better than they know anyone, but they do not. This makes them angry because they know their victims may soon be free from the prison they have built for them.

They reinforce their grip with hateful words with physical and mental abuse. They believe they are the solution for their victims and that no one would suspect a family member, a friend, a boyfriend, or a girlfriend because they put on masks of deception and smiles of kindness and love. They are enemies in disguise who plot against their victims.

Sometimes, abuse can kill a person quickly. The poison of choice can enter the person's soul without them realizing they have contracted a deadly virus.

It is like lighting a firecracker in a can and watching it blow up into millions of pieces. The victims may harm themselves because they think no one cares about them, and the only thing they can do is cry out for help in a destructive manner.

They do not think; they just act out. Sometimes, it has fatal consequences.

TAINTED COFFEE

Pour a cup of coffee,

Adding arsenic for that bittersweet taste,

Bringing death in every sip,

Slowly strangling the breath from the soul.

That was the purpose of your goal,

Killing life and any dream,

Hoping to keep me in that cold and dreary room.

As you fill my cup again,

Adding more of your arsenic friend,

Bury the voice,

Close the eyes,

Death!

Is what I see?

As you kill me with tainted coffee.

FINDING LIFE

Dying in a room

Four walls!

As darkness fills that place,

The tombs all set in a single line.

Hearing hatred,

Adding disgrace,

Leaving no flowers, no cards, no sign of life.

Just dust collects on that 9 to 5 address.

A tint of light shines into the space,

New breath captures the soul,

Adding resurrection to make it whole,

Walking out of my tomb

With no despair,

Escaping the hell that put me there.

UNWANTED FRIENDSHIP

Friendship I never knew,

Hatred filled the room.

As the fog blanketed the surface,

Heard unwanted words,

Burning the flesh like sulfuric acid,

Peeling away metal.

While the stench remain to remind the innocent,

Deceitful laughter strangles the soul.

Friends turn their backs,

As they watch, you die,

Consumed by all the lies,

Not knowing where to turn,

Wandering about the lessons learned.

RESURRECT

They tried to suffocate my soul,

Burying me in the bitter cold,

Hoping that darkness consumed me.

Dreams in my heart,

Crumbled,

Covered with hate.

That strangled my body,

Thinking that love died with me.

I cried out to someone.

No human being would hear my voices

So many rainbows of color,

Ran away.

Lying here in this unmarked grave

Until Jesus woke me up.

The doors opened,

I walked out and lived,

For truth, happiness, and joy

Are the gifts that make the Holy Father sing?

A SIMPLE PRAYER

As the wind blows,

Across the open fields,

Of despair,

I found myself disappear,

Floating in the clouds,

Watching beauty surrounds me.

With flowers, trees, and bumblebees,

So comforting,

Peaceful.

As God's angels watch over me.

Finding my way in this cold-hearted world,

Remembering the times that I was a girl,

Water splashing against the stone,

Wanting a new life to call my own.

TRUE LOVE

Do not leave me standing.

Alone!

Scared

And afraid,

Longing for a peaceful day,

Praying for answers from Heaven

Above,

Wanting to know the meaning of the

Truest love,

Not hating those who hurt me so,

Just needing that light to show,

Allowing God to change the soul.

Made anew.

That is the goal.

DESPERATE CRY

Did you hear my voice?

Crying within the wind,

Looking for freedom,

Longing to breathe a single breath.

That defines my life and career.

Right now, there's death living there.

With cobwebs on the windows,

Holes within the walls.

Life kept out.

Sunlight shimmering on the ice

As the keys lie on the floor,

Hoping for someone to open the door,

Taking me out of prison,

Into the light,

Saving my soul from the night

That is damp and cold.

SEEING THE BEAUTY

Finding a path

That leads to you.

Hearing the knowledge that saw

Me through.

Facing the truth that lies within.

Seeking hope and forgiveness from Him.

For you,

I breathe,

Seeing triumph among the grief,

There is hope within the soul.

In this world that is so cold,

Trying to keep away the tears,

Torment has endured for years,

Seeing the beauty here.

DYSFUNCTION

Did you hear the whispers in the night?

As the raindrops glistened bright,

A child said a prayer.

Hoping for love,

Believing in faith,

Wanting peace and joy,

In this place.

A world of hunger,

A world of hate,

Asking God about mistakes,

For two souls were fighting,

The third was dying.

From the pain that crept in the room

That led to their doom.

Wanting life and wisdom

Became a way of life.

DOMESTIC VIOLENCE

I sit looking out at the world,

There's so much pain and

Torment

That lies within the sand.

Seeing the tears on all those abused

Souls,

As each beating,

As each violent word,

Tears away the light in their lives.

The eyes are cold, and their bodies.

Prepared to die,

They lay on their beds for

The day to come,

Allowing violence to wrap around them like a blanket.

In the bitter cold

Who would hear that one soul?

On their knees crying out to be free?

A HEALER

Did you hear me?

As I called your name,

You told me.

I was to blame.

For your bitter shame,

Stop hiding!

Stop running!

I see your life.

Torn apart in so many pieces,

Cry daily,

For no reason.

Because my love is waiting,

Beside your wilted body.

Shivering!

Longing!

For wholeness.

That feeling that lies within.

Ask me, and I will forgive your sin.

A CHILD'S NIGHTMARE

You tried to hurt me.

Like so many days before.

Trying to even the score,

Since the day I was born.

Looking at the hate in your eyes,

All those nights you made me cry

Hitting—

Kicking—

Pulling my hair!

Letting family and friends abuse a soul.

Deprived and lacking love,

The world is so cold.

REALITY

Saw the hatred in your eyes,

Blaming me,

When things go wrong.

Hearing that same old pity-pat

Song.

Never calling!

Never asking!

What lies ahead in your life?

Tears I shed for you,

The day I died on the cross.

Lost and confused child,

When will you come back to me?

When will you ask to see?

One call,

And, I will set you free.

ABUSE WITHIN A FAMILY TREE

Looking beyond,

Seeing hate lying within a family tree,

Hateful words that kill the soul,

Crying in the bitter cold,

Alone and waiting for life,

Praying for change.

Tears fill the room.

As the family writes on my tomb,

"Not wanted or "No one wants you!"

The words buried in my heart,

No love from the start.

They prayed in silence,

Hoping I would never tell.

How their dreams for me were death and hell!

Now it must end,

Pruning off unwanted limbs.

PRINCESS

A child

Used and abused in the world,

I'll held you in my arms and give you strength.

Each tear shed from the pain and torture endured,

From the lies that tried to destroy.

I stopped them from living.

Gave peace within the mind,

Gave love when no one cared,

Gave life,

Began to live again.

Jesus Christ is the closest friend.

NEW CREATURE

Jesus Christ

Called me out from my tomb,

Breathing life back into my soul.

A new creature has risen from the dead,

No longer bound by blindness, deafness,

Or the sense of giving up.

The eyes are beautiful windows,

When I walk,

He holds my hand,

The words he spoke into life.

Have grown like a flower,

In fertilized soul.

SAVE ME

Rock away the sorrow,

Walk away the pain,

Jesus!

You called my name.

Heard it in the wind,

So gentle and mild.

Knew I was his child.

Wept in the cold,

Wept in the darkness,

Tried to find my way,

Waited patiently.

Until I called his name,

"Jesus! Come save me!"

I'M RIGHT HERE!

You called last night,

Did you hear me?

Were you hiding in fear?

Child!

Don't you understand?

I died on the cross

To show that you are not left behind.

Step out,

Follow me.

To the completion that a Father can give,

With the promise that life will change.

HELPLESS SOUL

Beauty withers up,

Like a flower cut from the vine.

Teardrops of disgrace, ugliness, and loneliness fill the mind.

Each drop that falls,

You relive the awful pain,

As a wardrobe of shame,

Smothers your every breath,

No one hears the voice inside you,

Helpless soul,

Nowhere to turn.

Don't you see the lesson learned!

Jesus died on Calvary so we could be free.

Lay your burdens down,

Life can come now.

DON'T LEAVE ME HERE

I hear your voice.

Calling my name,

Whispering through the wind and rain,

For I have fallen.

Pick me up.

Out of the darkness.

It is cold and dreary.

Here.

No doors or windows.

Do I see?

Just a coffin covering me.

Take me someplace.

To see the light,

Heaven is what I mean.

Beauty shines there,

Bright and pure,

Sacred love

That draws my soul.

Jesus lifts me up and makes me whole.

ONE DAY

Waiting by the sea,

No one noticed me,

Words of hate said…

As the tears flood my bed,

Drowning in past lies,

People laughing all around.

Hoping I died in the next room,

Telling friends spells of glory,

Because they only heard their story.

As they sell their souls for trinkets and gold,

Jesus came and made me whole.

WANTING AN ANSWER

Coldness is what I felt,

Surrounded by the darkness,

Trying to capture my soul,

Needing to get out of the four walls.

Climbed to the light,

Scarred with those harmful words,

Spit dripping from my hair.

The footprints on my back,

The dried teardrops on my cheeks.

Wanting,

Longing for hope to come my way.

Someone saved me,

Love me for who I am,

Stopping the abuse that taunts from the cracks of the broken

China,

Bringing life back into the tormented soul.

LAYING THAT VERBAL ABUSE AT THE CROSS

Tears fell rapidly on my pillow.

As the pain ran so deep,

Did anyone care about my feelings?

As those cold words cut my soul inside,

Trying to destroy life, I held so dear.

"If only I tried a little more."

Were the words of a broken heart?

No human could endure,

Salvation was the cure.

Life support keeps me alive.

It is faith that keeps love inside.

Dysfunction was all I knew,

Longing to hear the truth,

No more lying, crying, and verbal abuse!

LOST SOUL HEAR MY VOICE

Why do you hate, me so?

Was it the fact that I died on the cross?

So that my blood can wash

Away your sins.

Or for my love for everyone?

Forgiving one's soul.

I know all your names.

I Cry when you do wrong.

I can heal your pain.

Only if you ask me.

I will care for you.

When no one is there,

I will live within you,

Don't you know!

Jesus Christ is here.

LOOKING FROM HEAVEN'S WINDOW

Draw near to me,

I will keep you safe from harm.

You will find the answers you need.

Only if you believe.

No one knows you the way I do,

Timid soul,

Lost and afraid.

Crying out from the tormented grave,

Wanting love that only I could fulfill,

Longing for truth that only I could give.

Your pain has kept you away.

The lies dug your grave.

I am waiting for you to call my name,

Your tears have shed your shame.

DEAR DIARY, THE BEGINNING

Dear Diary,

I Lived a bitter life.

Not caring.

Time ticks,

Watching and sitting as hours go by.

How did I let all those men lie?

Never listening to my soul,

Almost died of the bitter cold.

Somehow, love disappeared,

The abuse was so clear.

Yearning and tired of being alone,

Falling on my knees, crying.

Saved on that dark and dreary day,

Feeling a love worth more than words,

Holding onto my ray of light,

Despite the past.

Learning to love again.

Never fearing what might lie ahead,

His eyes are fiery red.

Just one look and you will know,

Jesus is not dead.

REBIRTH

Here I sit:

Joy, peace, and happiness

Sine within my soul.

No time to worry about the past.

Finally, free at last,

I know that love soothes my heart,

Making whole once again.

Since Jesus became my friend.

The road is rough,

But it is okay.

No need to cry.

I am not afraid.

THANKFUL

Hope you are blessed.

By what is said.

Say your prayers

Before you go to bed.

God said, "There will be brighter days.

And all your troubles, I'll take away."

Blessed to hear the call,

After all,

You have much to thank Him,

SLIVERS OF GLASS

Destruction.

On all their minds.

Destroying the family tree,

Time after time.

When will it end?

They have no friends.

Slivers of glass.

All over the ground,

Spreading unlawful rumors,

All over town.

No speaking.

No love.

No tears

They cry.

Could not care less if the family member died.

The slivers of glass,

Still lay on the ground.

SEARCHING

Never knew real love.

Never was I allowed to fit in.

Choices that people made for me.

Why won't they let me live!

It seems like darkness,

A voice imprisoned,

There is no way out.

Pray for answers.

Knowing that help is on the way,

Angels come to my rescue;

Needed them the most.

Our Heavenly Father also

Sent the Holy Ghost.

TEARDROP

Life exists only.

In the time spent

Alone,

Wondering about

Decisions.

That must be

Made,

Did you know?

How much time

Goes by

Once all the loneliness

Has passed

And that last teardrop

Dries?

Ways change day by day.

All the hardship just

Dies away.

MY LIFE

You gave me hope.

With words of promise.

Started living.

And understanding

My purpose in life.

No need to worry.

About my past.

Finally, free

To let it go.

Nothing

Made me live that way.

Glad that it did not stay.

No tears

Will I shed?

No more staying

In bed.

Someone finally noticed me.

No lies,

Truth in each word,

Seeing past looks and sex appeal.

Say how I feel.

No running!

No hiding!

Must take a chance,

Knowing God has sent to me,

Spirit so pure

That dwells in me.

WHISPERING WILLOWS

Whispering Willows told,

The future of destruction and despair.

People still party without

A care.

Claiming my salvation is

Where I want to be,

Knowing I'll be set free.

Whispering Willows told me about Jesus,

Healing the sick.

Being cured of all my illnesses

Is what I want for me.

Jesus! Jesus!

Set me free.

Whispering Willows

Told about heaven and

Earth being as one.

Book of Revelations makes it clear,

Listen to the Whispering Willows,

Because that time is here.

WORLD'S BIGGEST CRIME

Sitting by the window,

Watching the world around Me.

Sadness,

Madness,

Hatred,

Love.

No one listening.

Afraid of touch.

A kind word,

Which we call love.

Did you see my eyes?

Did you see my face?

Filled with sadness for

The human race.

Never getting better,

Always getting worse as days go by.

Money cannot buy happiness.

Broken-hearted and filled

With pain,

Hoping the world will change.

EYES

Eyes are windows

To the spirit, that dwells,

Within.

Looking,

Connecting

One spirit to another.

Awakening,

No words said.

Blessed

By a miracle,

Saved by grace,

Each holding the Lord's hands.

Believing

Happiness can come.

Filling broken hearts with love.

Stop crying,

Seeing the Lord's face and eyes.

DEAR JESUS

Dear Jesus,

Watch over my brother.

Tears of innocence,

He confessed,

Waiting for truth.

Protect him from harm,

His body beaten.

His faith has dwindled in despair.

Please,

Send angels to tell him.

How much you care.

WE ARE ALL GOD'S CHILDREN

We are all God's children

Standing tall,

With guardian angels watching us all,

For each problem.

Solved with

Tender loving care.

That is how I know God is always there.

Although, I might not be perfect in

Every way.

I care enough to live each day.

I shout out to anyone to hear my story.

I am not looking for fame and glory.

God listens to all our prayers.

Men and women look to God with tears,

Finding the answers to all those lies,

Realizing God loves us all.

That is why we are all God's children.

Stand tall.

6' UNDER

Abuse kills silently,

Killing a nation with words.

Empty shells that walk the earth,

Watching tears fill their eyes.

With no love or compassion for man.

There is no hope.

Told there could never be joy.

No life to fill an open door.

Just a dream of loneliness,

A coffin made from hate

And despair.

We dwell in chains of darkness,

Looking for a light,

To shine.

SKELETON IN THE CLOSET

Haunted by the past,

Many secrets locked away,

Family unknown.

HIBERNATING

A set of snowflakes,

A white blanket lies

On the ground.

As the winter slips in,

No life forms around found.

SECRET 2

Truth goes untold.

Many are hurt along the way.

Lives are destroyed.

FORGOTTEN HERITAGE

I see you wander from place to place,

Not knowing where you belong.

No one is honest about the situation,

Lost as time goes past by.

Will not be told.

Afraid of telling something so vital,

A family destroyed by such fate.

Grandmother, tell me the secret that you hold.

SECRET 3

Childhood hurt;

Heritage locked away,

Opened with a key.

BARBIE DOLL SYNDROME

A false beauty,

Preserved with surgeries,

At a certain price.

VINTAGE YEARS

Looking at beauty

Gray hair, wrinkles, bifocals.

Wisdom with age.

THIS ISN'T HEAVEN

Aging at a horrific speed

Gray hair, bifocals, wrinkles, out-of-shape figure,

Misplaced false teeth,

Wearing

Depend on diapers daily,

Children fighting over the assets

(No one's dead)

Getting held up by the denture grip,

Buying a plot that overlooks a city dump,

Forced to live in a nursing home,

Waiting for a date with the Grim Reaper.

Just give me a one-way ticket out of hell.

PEACE

Once so lonely

In my heart

Not knowing where I had to be,

Still,

Had to face.

Reality.

Each tear I shed,

Jesus knew the pain.

He filled my heart

Made it whole.

He brought me out

Of death's range,

Telling me certain things,

True and pure,

Here to proclaim

Gave him all the glory.

He died for you and me.

It is great living with his peace.

WAKE UP & SMELL REALITY

Always told I could never have,

Or could never be.

Words of torment running so free,

As it killed my soul.

No matter where I turned,

Or where I looked,

Could not escape those horrifying words.

Longing for life,

Longing for truth,

Seeing the world,

Crying since I was a girl.

Wanting to be free,

From hate,

That surrounds me.

SOUL

Spirit lying in the flesh,

Tempted to sin,

Needing to be saved from within

Cannot express the love I have.

Jesus, Thank you!

For coming to my rescue.

BEYOND

Lost in a bottle of despair,

Thinking that there is no one there.

The time has come to tell the story,

But you allowed the devil to steal your glory.

Trapped by spirit and nothing else,

Walking around pitying yourself.

Tired of hearing the same old line,

Allow Jesus to ease your mind.

PENNIES ON THE TABLE

Money,

Rusted and old,

Tempting to the soul.

Can leave you lying there,

But it always seems to disappear.

Some people fight for your love,

Can't hold me!

Can't have my heart!

Smelling like the many lovers,

You had in your mist,

Having their affection and their kiss.

NAPKIN FILLED WITH STAINS

Open the door,

So, the light can come in.

Your dwelling

Filled with cobwebs,

Dust,

Dishes undone.

Not taking notice of the furniture

Falling,

Falling apart!

Like the abuse has done

To the heart.

Snap out of it!

Snap out of it!

When will you learn?

Leave troubles behind.

FUTURE BRINGS

A dream is a goal that has not,

Yet been fulfilled!

When fulfilled,

It will be conquered!

CAN I GET A LITTLE ARSENIC WITH THAT?

The only friendship that I know,

Abusive in its entire glow,

Feeling like arsenic flowing through my veins,

Choking the breath out of me.

My eyes blinded by the lies,

As they stuck daggers in my eyes.

Watching as my soul dies,

Torture and torment persist,

Knowing I will never be missed.

Trying to keep me in my tomb,

In that dark and secluded room

Filled with hate.

Death holds the key

For those enemies

Who have tried to poison me.

www.ingramcontent.com/pod-product-compliance
Lightning Source LLC
Chambersburg PA
CBHW051324120626
46547CB00015B/2386